Contents

Vitamin D Explained:

The Incredible, Healing Powers of Sunlight

By C.K. Murray

Copyright © 2014 C.K. Murray

Similar works by C.K. Murray:

The Wonders of Water: How H2O Can Transform Your Life

High Blood Pressure Explained: Natural, Effective, Drug-Free Treatment for the "Silent Killer"

Natural Weight Loss: PROVEN Strategies for Healthy Weight Loss & Accelerated Metabolism

Master Mind: Unleashing the Infinite Power of the Latent Brain

Mindfulness Explained: The Mindful Solution to Stress, Depression, and Chronic Unhappiness

Emotional Intelligence Explained: How to Master Emotional Intelligence and Unlock Your True Ability

The Sun.

It's the reason Earth is inhabitable. Without sunlight, plants would not grow, humans would not prosper, and our impressive planet would be just another rock floating in space. Basically, the sun is the building block of life. *All* life. And sunlight, our greatest source of Vitamin D, is quite literally our life *stream*.

Take a look around you. What do you see? Chances are there's sunshine, somewhere. Maybe the weather is bad and overcast, or maybe that bright, glorious yellow is bursting through. No matter the atmosphere or temperature, we *all* stand to gain from vitamin D.

Did you know that vitamin D actually changes the way our genes express themselves? That it literally touches almost every cell in our body? No joke. In fact, the latest studies reveal that vitamin D can *dramatically* improve diabetes, cardiovascular
disease and hypertension, infections, immune functioning, autoimmune disorders, neuropsychological functioning, and even cancer.

But there's a problem. Most of us are not getting enough, and it's showing.

Let's be honest, we're busy. We're plugged in and hooked up to our technologies today like never before. We've got issues at work, and bills to pay, and kids to deal with, and friends to see, and family functions, and a million other things that consume our time and crowd our minds. Too many times we're stuck indoors, in offices and homes and apartments and schools and shops and malls and restaurants and cars and trucks and—the list goes on!

Simply put, most of us are missing out, and we don't even realize it. The facts speak for themselves: organizations like the World Health Organization (WHO) and the Center for Disease Control (CDC) now estimate that over 1 *billion* people worldwide are "D-ficient." While being deficient in one category of vitamins may not seem like a big deal, the negative effects are alarming. In fact, researchers are now calling vitamin D deficiency a global 'pandemic.' With the resurgence of rickets, a bone-weakening disease once believed eradicated, vitamin D fortification has become more pressing than ever.

The bottom line is simple: vitamin D is a critical source of good health and vitality. And as the studies pour out, its numerous powers continue to wow us.

Chapter 1 – What Exactly *Is* Vitamin D?

Vitamin D is in many ways the most studied and confusing topic in the recent history of the nutrition world. As deficiency, at-risk, and recommended levels of vitamin D have changed, so too have the commonly held opinions of the vitamin. Although researchers still argue over how to categorize the vitamin, one thing is certain: vitamin D is no normal vitamin. Although it is commonly called a vitamin, it is actually both a steroid hormone and a nutrient. It is a substance that is synthesized from sunlight, as opposed to most 'essential dietary vitamins' which are derived solely from an organism's diet. With vitamin D, the process is quite complex, but one that is necessary for us to continue living healthy lives.

When ultraviolet radiation (UVB) rays hit your skin, a chemical reaction occurs. Your body begins the process of converting your skin's *prohormone*, or precursor to a hormone, to vitamin D. A form of naturally-occurring cholesterol called 7-dehydrocholesterol (7-DHC) then absorbs the UVB radiation and gets converted into cholecalciferol, the previtamin form of D3. After this, the previtamin goes through the bloodstream to your liver, where the body metabolizes it and turns it into hydroxyvitamin D. The kidneys then convert the hydroxyvitamin D3 into dihydroxyvitamin D3, the hormone form of vitamin D that your body can use.

Basically, vitamin D absorption all begins with that first touch of ultra violet rays on your skin. From there, your body's internal processes affect the extent to which that vitamin D is accurately metabolized and utilized.

Understanding how your body produces vitamin D is of utmost importance. By knowing the factors that contribute to vitamin D deficiency, we all can enjoy the amazing powers of the sunshine vitamin.

Chapter 2 – What's Holding You Back? Reasons You Aren't Getting Enough Vitamin D

There are multiple reasons why we might be deficient in vitamin D. Fortunately, most of them are easily treated simply by exposing ourselves to more sunlight, or by taking supplementation. Here are the most common reasons, and what you can do to overcome them:

Reason # 1: Skin Color: Skin pigmentation plays a huge role in the absorption of sunlight and production of vitamin D. The darker the skin color, the more difficult it is for that skin to produce vitamin D. Skin pigmentation is a natural sunscreen that filters out UVB radiation. Basically, if you have darker skin, you need to expose yourself to more sunlight. You may also want to consider supplementation.

Reason # 2: Sunscreen: Like your pigmentation, sunscreen also blocks UVB rays from the sun. Although this is good for fighting pre-mature skin aging and skin cancer, it makes it much harder to get the vitamin D you need. Try using a weaker SPF or using more sunscreen on problem areas like your face and neck while applying less to your arms and legs. Remember, too much sunscreen has also been shown in some studies to clog your pours and actually exacerbate skin problems. Consult your dermatologist for a plan that works for you.

Reason #3: Body Fat: Because vitamin D is a fat-soluble vitamin, it gets stored in your fat. While this initially seems like a good thing, it isn't. If vitamin D is in your fat, it isn't in your blood. The more fat in your body, the more vitamin D deposited in that fat, leading to less vitamin D in your circulation and thus decreasing bioavailability. It's no surprise then that many studies strongly correlate vitamin D deficiency with obesity.

In fact, obesity in *children* is especially a problem.

People who struggle with fat absorption will certainly struggle with vitamin D intake. Such conditions include deficiency of the pancreatic enzymes, cystic fibrosis, celiac disease (gluten intolerance), crohn's disease, particular types of liver disease, and the surgical removal portions or all of the stomach or intestine. If any of these conditions are present, supplementation is your best option, in accordance with your physician's recommended treatment plan.

Reason # 4: Not Enough Milk: Milk is an important dietary agent of change when it comes to getting enough vitamin D. People at risk include children and teens who don't get sun and don't drink at least 2 cups of vitamin D-fortified milk per day. Furthermore, people who are lactose intolerant, allergic to milk, or simply don't like milk products will also be at risk for deficiency. Even infants, who are breast-fed only, will be at risk. However, if that infant is switched over to 2 cups of formula per day, an adequate level is met. Natural breast milk surely has its benefits, but do not underestimate the importance of formula.

Reason # 5: Geography and Season: In the summer, lounging around the pull or sun-basking is a good way to get vitamin D. However, during the fall and winter, people who live at higher latitudes have to deal with the low angle of the sun in the sky. This may mean that people at such altitudes literally get no vitamin D. In the northern hemisphere, people living in Boston, Edmonton, and parts of Norway can't get enough vitamin D for up to 6 months of the year. In the southern hemisphere, people in parts of Argentina and South Africa get little to no vitamin D from the sun during their winter months. Although the body stores vitamin D from summer sun exposure, by wintertime, most people in these geographic locations are already deficient. Be wary of where you live. Try to enjoy the sun as much as your skin allows, without getting sunburnt. Take vacations to different locales. Embrace a lifestyle that allows greater outdoors activities. Don't be afraid of some sun—just don't go overboard.

Remember, there are always alternatives to sunlight. Say for instance, a tanning bed. Now, now, many people decry tanning beds for their potential to contribute to cancer, but this *can* be avoided. Most tanning equipment use magnetic ballasts that not only generate light, but also EMF fields, which can contribute to cancer. Try to avoid these types of tanning beds. If you hear a loud buzzing noise while in a tanning bed, it is generating an EMF field. It is best to use tanning beds that employ *electronic* ballasts.

Just be sure that the tanning bed you're using is emitting UVB radiation, as many simply put out UVA (the main cause of tanning and skin damage). The higher the UV*B* output, the better. UVB is of medium-wavelength and cannot penetrate beyond the superficial skin layers. Much of the solar UVB rays can be caught by the atmosphere, making sunshine exposure that much more important. By contrast, the relatively long-wavelength UVA makes up roughly 95 percent of the UV radiation hitting the Earth's surface, and contributes the most to skin ageing and wrinkling. UVA is also the main culprit in skin cancer.

Reason #6: Age: Aging drastically reduces the body's ability to produce vitamin D because the kidneys are less able to make the conversion. Studies now reveal that a healthy 70 year old person makes as much as *4 times* less vitamin D than a healthy 20 year old.

If your elderly loved one spends too much time indoors in their home, apartment, or retirement residence, be sure to encourage outdoor leisure—if possible. Gardening and sitting on a porch are simple but enjoyable activities that will do wonders for you elderly loved ones. If this individual is ridden with health problems and cannot feasibly make it outside, consider supplementation. The proper levels of supplementation will be explained later in Chapter 6. Just remember, if your elders do elect to spend leisure time sitting on a porch, make sure to avoid a glass screen. The body cannot make any vitamin D when exposed to sunlight through glass since glass filters out most of the UVB that stimulates vitamin D production.

Reason # 7: Air Pollution: The stuff in the air matters a big deal. When carbon particulates from the burning of fossil fuels, wood, and other materials get in the atmosphere, they readily absorb UVB rays. Big urban areas with smog and pollution may make it very difficult for UVB rays to get down to our flesh. Ironically, ozone absorbs UVB radiation, so the deterioration of the ozone layer may be a pollution issue that actually ends up boosting vitamin D levels.

Now that you know about the reasons why you might be deficient, it's time to know what exactly indicates deficiency. If you know the signs, then you know to act. And the sooner you act, the sooner you will begin to experience a variety of amazing health benefits. After all, vitamin D is now considered one of the most powerful health hacks for modern living. So what are you waiting for?

Chapter 3 – Why You Can't Afford to Wait. Symptoms of "D-ficiency" and How to Treat Them

Once upon a time, a time not too long ago, little was known about vitamin D. Doctors and specialists assumed that occasional sunlight when possible was enough, and that vitamin D, like any vitamin, was just a small piece of the puzzle. However, as years passed and other health ailments cropped up, experts everywhere realized something. Vitamin D is *not* just another vitamin, and it is *not* just something we can blow off from time to time. In fact, the National Health and Nutrition Examination Survey found that 50 percent of American children from one to five years old, and 70 percent of children from six to 11, are deficient in vitamin D. Researchers estimate that 50 percent of the general population is at risk of vitamin D deficiency.

Here are some basic symptoms to look out for in case you are vitamin D deficient and don't know it:

Fatigue

General muscle pain and weakness

Chronic pain

Poor concentration

Headaches

Weight gain

High blood pressure

Muscle cramps

Joint pain

Restless sleep

Bladder problems

Constipation or diarrhea

Overall, the medical consensus now finds that failure to get enough vitamin D has been attributed to conditions vastly more serious than the aforementioned symptoms. Thankfully, by simply getting more of the vitamin through supplementation or lifestyle changes, we can all dramatically reduce all of these conditions. And in doing so, we can enjoy health benefits we never thought possible.

Chapter 4 – 12 Amazing Medical Benefits of the Sunshine Vitamin

Did you know that vitamin D affects over 3,000 genes in a positive way? Did you know that vitamin D can literally restructure our genetic code and change the efficiency and potency of our cells on a day to day, minute to minute, second to second basis? Well now you do. Let's take a look at what the vitamin can do specifically:

Diabetes - A Finnish study focusing on 10,366 children found that when given 2000 international units (IU)/day of vitamin D3 per day during their first year of life, the children experience amazing benefits. The children were studied for 31 years afterwards, and the risk of type 1 diabetes was diminished by almost 80 percent. Research has also shown that constant optimal levels of vitamin D reduces the risk of type 2 diabetes, as well as the symptoms of both preexisting types. When combined with a heart healthy regimen, the results are significant.

Respiratory Illness – Lower respiratory tract infections are the leading cause of death among all infectious diseases. The most well-known are bronchitis and pneumonia, causing cough, chest pain and fever in alarming numbers. Influenza infections affect both the upper and lower respiratory tracts, but the most virulent strains, such as H1N1, bury deep in the lower lungs and can cause severe symptoms, even death. Fortunately multiple meta-analyses of vitamin D find that the vitamin helps to greatly reduce the development and sustenance of such illnesses.

Muscle weakness – Ever feel sore or tired? Ever feel a dull ache all over, like your body is just beat up and giving up? Experts now realize that muscle weakness is often caused by vitamin D deficiency, and that many symptoms of this deficiency are misdiagnosed as fibromyalgia or chronic fatigue syndrome. Feeling tired and achy is a normal wintertime complaint that can lead to osteoporosis if not treated with vitamin D. Without the vitamin, the body struggles to put calcium into your skeletal muscles and structure, thus contributing to a throbbing, deep-seated bone pain.

Bone problems – Calcium and vitamin D are important foundations for ensuring your bone density and strength. Vitamin D helps promote the absorption of calcium from the intestines. Without enough vitamin D, the bones become calcium-depleted (osteomalacia), which can lead to cracks and fractures. Vitamin D, in conjunction with a healthy, calcium-rich diet may greatly reduce the risk of osteoporosis.

Chronic kidney disease – The kidney is an essential part of the body's vitamin D conversion and utilization process. Patients with advanced chronic kidney diseases (especially requiring dialysis) are unable to produce the active form of vitamin D. By taking supplements, these individuals will drastically reduce the risk of renal bone disease as well as regulate hormone levels, thus preventing the body from pulling calcium out of the bones and weakening them.

Asthma - Vitamin D may help control the symptoms and attacks associated with asthma. Currently patients with severe asthma take certain steroid tablets or inhalers—unfortunately, some types of asthma are resistant to these steroids. Many studies including those in Japan and London found that asthma attacks in school children were significantly lowered in those who took a daily vitamin D supplement of 1200 International Units (IU) per day. In a review of roughly 60 years' worth of literature on vitamin D, experts find that vitamin D deficiency is linked to increased airway reactivity, reduced lung functioning, and diminished control.

Psoriasis - Roughly 7.5 million Americans have psoriasis, a chronic, inflammatory disease that leads to itchy, scaly patches on the skin. It is largely believed that the scaly patches occur because the immune system incorrectly identifies healthy cells as dangerous ones and triggers a defensive protein that causes inflammations. Vitamin D is believed to inhibit this inflammatory response and lead to greater overall skin health.

Periodontal issues - Chronic gum disease is not only a cosmetic problem by causing swelling and bleeding, but is also a very real threat to other parts of your body. Fortunately vitamin D has been shown to increase defensins and cathelicidin, compounds that lower the number of bacteria in the mouth and boost your mouth's natural immunities.

Cardiovascular disease – Like skeletal muscle, the heart is a big muscle that has vitamin D receptors. Congestive heart failure and other heart problems have been regularly associated with vitamin D deficiency. Research conducted at *Harvard University* found that women with low vitamin D levels had a 67 percent increase in their risk of developing hypertension. At Boston University, people with high blood pressure who were exposed to UVA and UVB rays for three months found that their vitamin D levels increased by over 100%, *and* their high blood pressure normalized. Vitamin D is believed to reduce the production of a hormone called renin, which likely plays a central role in hypertension.

In another important piece of research, the Health Professional Follow-Up Study assessed the blood levels of vitamin D in almost 50,000 men who were healthy, and then continued to assess them periodically over 10 years. The longitudinal study found that men who were deficient in vitamin D were twice as likely to have a heart attack as men with adequate levels. Other studies discovered that low vitamin D levels are significantly correlated with higher risk of heart failure, sudden cardiac death, stroke, overall cardiovascular disease, and cardiovascular death. In the end, experts argue that vitamin D plays an important role in controlling blood pressure and preventing artery damage.

Schizophrenia and Depression – Not only have studies linked these disorders to vitamin D deficiency, but now, newer studies have shown that regular vitamin D levels may delay or even prevent the onset of the disorders. Vitamin D is believed to regulate and normalize neurotransmitters in the brain. In fact, Seasonal Affective Disorder (SAD) is linked directly to lower levels of sunlight exposure. The associations between schizophrenia and vitamin D are also very telling:

Most patients with schizophrenia are vitamin D deficient

Schizophrenia varies with latitude

Schizophrenia is more common in those with dark skin

Schizophrenia has increased around the world as vitamin D intake has decreased

Schizophrenia is linked to lower natal vitamin D

Schizophrenia is linked to low birth rates, which are linked to low vitamin D levels, *and*

Schizophrenia is linked to Autism which is linked to low vitamin D levels

Let it be known that many studies have also associated vitamin D deficiency to a whole slew of neurological and cognitive problems. Everything from cognitive decline to schizophrenia, psychopathy, Alzheimer's, dementia, multiple sclerosis, and Parkinson's. ADHD is also a result of decreased vitamin D and increased time spent indoors.

Cancer - Researchers at *Georgetown University Medical Center* in Washington DC have found a connection between high vitamin D intake and reduced risk of breast cancer. Presented at the *American Association for Cancer Research*, the findings revealed that higher doses of vitamin were linked to a 75 percent reduction in overall cancer growth and a 50 percent reduction in tumor cases among current cancer patients. Another prominent study in the Nurses' Health Studies indicated that nurses with the highest blood levels of vitamin D, about 50 ng/ml, cut their chance of getting breast cancer by as much as 50 percent.

Similarly, a Canadian study showed that women who reported having the *most* sun exposure as teenagers and young adults had nearly a 70 percent reduced risk of developing breast cancer. In another study published in the *Journal of the American Medical Association* in 2003, of over 3,000 veterans (ages 50 to 75) at 13 Veterans Affairs medical centers, those took in more than 645 IU of vitamin D per day had a 40% reduction in their risk of developing precancerous colon polyps.

A more recent 4-year randomized study in 2007 looked at 1,179 healthy women over age 55. A third of the women were given 1,400 to 1,500 milligrams of calcium each day. Another third received calcium in addition 1,100 IU of vitamin D3 every day, and the final third simply got a placebo. In the end, the women who took calcium and vitamin D had a dramatically lowered risk for all types of cancer, as did the women who started the study with higher vitamin D levels

DNA and metabolic revival – On the level of genetic material, vitamin D has been found to have a tremendous impact. One pertinent study showed that healthy volunteers taking 2,000 IU's of vitamin D per day for several months increased the efficacy of 291 different genes that control as much as 80 various metabolic processes. In laymen's terms, vitamin D improved DNA repair, boosted the immune system, and streamlined countless other biological processes.

An important biomarker of age and vitality is that of the telomere. Telomeres are caps at the end of chromosomes that protect the DNA from damage. Telomeres decrease in length with each cell division until there is nothing left, at which point the cells die or undergo a permanent arrest, known as senescence. Basically, the younger you are the longer your telomere length.

A large epidemiological study of 2,100 female twin pairs found that elevated vitamin D levels correlated with increased telomere length in white blood cells. The difference in telomere length between vitamin D sufficient pairs versus vitamin D insufficient pairs accounted for 5 years of aging. Those that regularly supplemented with vitamin D had longer telomeres and aged slower than those that did not. In many ways, vitamin D is quite literally a lifesaver. Not to mention, a major contributor to mindful living.

Again, in terms of the diseases associated with vitamin D deficiency, be wary of:

Osteoporosis and Osteopenia

Alzheimer's Disease

Bursitis

Gout

17 varieties of Cancer (breast, prostate and colon, etc.)

Heart disease

High blood pressure

Obesity

Metabolic Syndrome and Diabetes

Chronic fatigue syndrome

Fibromyalgia

Chronic Pain

Autoimmune diseases

Depression and Seasonal Affective Disorder

Periodontal disease

Psoriasis

Multiple sclerosis

Rheumatoid arthritis

Osteoarthritis

Infertility and PMS

Parkinson's Disease

Now that you have familiarized yourself with some of the symptoms and diseases associated with "D-ficiency," you are ready to tackle the next topic. That is, how do we *ensure*, beyond a shred of doubt, that we are getting the right amount of vitamin D for our unique bodies? How can we ensure that we are 'optimizing' our blood levels of vitamin D?

Well, the answer is easier than you think. And one of the most important things to remember aside from getting sunlight—and especially if you aren't yet taking supplements—is to eat the right foods.

Chapter 5 – Eat Up! Sun-Rich Foods that Fuel the Fire

First and foremost, vitamin D should be received from the sun. But this isn't always an easy task. That's why there are alternatives. Now, by this point you know that Vitamin D supplements are very important, especially for those who are already deficient. But what about foods?

Did you know that there are several delicious, widely available foods that can jack up your blood levels and make your sunlight requirements that much easier?

Although vitamin D does not occur naturally in most foods, the recent medical focus on the vitamin's powers has led to an entire movement of D-fortification. Nowadays, especially in the American diet, many foods are enhanced with Vitamin D. This fortification is a good thing, but still may not be enough. This is why we need to balance enriched foods with sun exposure and possible supplementation. Most experts recommended 2,000 – 4,000 International Units (IU). For now, here is a quick list of foods that are rich in vitamin D: They are also great for natural weight loss.

Beef or calf liver

Egg yolks – These bad-boys have 4-6 times more vitamin D than conventional eggs. Eat up!

Canned sardines in oil – Easy to make and great for snacks, or side-meals any time of day. They also have omega 3 fatty acids, B vitmains and amino acids which are great for a healthy body and mind.

Milk or yogurt – regardless of fat content and fortification

Cheese

Salmon (preferably wild)

Mackerel (preferably wild-caught that are low in mercury) – Just like salmon, jam-packed with vitamin D. The American Heart Association recommends eating fatty, oily fish twice a week.

Mushrooms exposed to ultraviolet light

Vitamin D Values of Mushrooms	
Mushroom Type	Vitamin D Content (IU)
Mushrooms, brown, Italian, or Crimini, raw	3
Mushrooms, chanterelle, raw	178
Mushrooms, enoki, raw	4
Mushrooms, maitake, raw	943
Mushrooms, morel, raw	173

Mushrooms, oyster, raw	24
Mushrooms, portabella, raw	8
Mushrooms, portabella, exposed to UV rays, grilled	493
Mushrooms, portabella, exposed to UV rays, raw	375
Mushrooms, portabella, grilled	12
Mushrooms, shiitake, raw	15
Mushrooms, shiitake, cooked with salt	24
Mushrooms, shiitake, cooked without salt	24
Mushrooms, shiitake, dried	129
Mushrooms, shiitake, stir-fried	18
Mushrooms, white, raw	6
Mushrooms, white, cooked, boiled, drained with salt	7
Mushrooms, white, cooked, boiled, drained without salt	7

| Mushrooms, white, microwaved | 9 |
| Mushrooms, white, stir-fried | 7 |

Cod liver oil -- This is the number one food source for vitamin D. It remains one of the best ways to build up immunity and get your daily D dose.

Tuna canned in water

Basically, fish are great for you, as are dairy products. Just be wary of how you prepare them. You will lose some vitamin D from foods cooked in oil, as much as 20% from fried eggs, and 10% from the poaching process. Fortunately, vitamin D is very stable over time. In fact, there is no significant loss of vitamin D from cheese even a year after ripening. That said, most of the best sources of vitamin D such as fish, eggs, and milk should be consumed while fresh. In other words, enjoy vitamin D, but don't do so at the expense of the other nutrients in these healthy foods. Again: balance, balance, *balance*!

And that balance is what will take you from feeling like crap to walking on clouds. According to the National Institutes of Health (NIH), the aforementioned foods contain roughly this amount of IUs (International Units):

Foods Rich in Vitamin D

Cod liver oil, 1 tablespoon	1360 IU
Swordfish, cooked, 3 ounces	566 IU
Salmon (sockeye), cooked, 3 ounces	447 IU
Tuna fish, canned in water, drained, 3 ounces	154 IU
Orange juice fortified with vitamin D, 1 cup	137 IU
Milk, nonfat, reduced fat, and whole, vitamin D fortified, 1 cup	115-124 IU
Yogurt, fortified with 20% of the DV for vitamin D, 6 ounces	80 IU
Margarine, fortified, 1 tablespoon	60 IU
Sardines, canned in oil, two sardines	46 IU
Liver, beef, cooked, 3 ounces	42 IU
Egg, 1 large (vitamin D in yolk)	41 IU
Cereal, fortified with 10% of the DV for vitamin D, 075-1 cup	40 IU
Cheese, Swiss, 1 ounce	6 IU

This may seem all good and well, but now it begs a new question: How many IUs do we need?

Chapter 6 – Optimizing Your Intake—Supplements and Blood Levels

Obviously, getting the vitamin D you need depends on a lot of factors. Your weight, your bodily processes, and even your location on the Earth all relate to how easy or difficult vitamin D intake will be. But even so, how do we know *just* how much we really need? For the longest time, physicians, specialists, and researchers have argued over the exact right amount for the general public. Although these blood levels are typically expressed in ranges, the ranges can vary. Just decades prior, these ranges were much lower. Today, though, with all the knowledge we have garnered, the difference is telling.

However, before we get into the precise blood levels of vitamin D, it is important to understand how those levels are measured and expressed.

When we talk about vitamin D blood levels, we refer to them in terms of ng/ml. This refers to how many nanograms per milliliter of the active *25-hydroxydivitamin D3* we have in our body. If you're wondering what your levels are like, there is actually an App for it here.

You can also get an exact reading by asking your doctor for a vitamin D test. Specifically, a 25(OH)D test—which just might be covered by your health insurance. You can also order an in-home test, which pricks your finger and puts a drop of blood on blotter paper. You then send the paper to a lab to be tested. This is an alternative to going to a doctor or having to deal with your insurance company. Finally, you can elect to order a test online and get blood work done at a laboratory. In the United States, there are several websites that allow you to bypass your doctor such as mymedlab.com, healthcheckusa.com and privatemdlabs.com.

Let it be known that the optimal level for vitamin D is commonly considered 40-60 ng/ml. You can calculate how many International Units (IU) this takes based on your weight by using the following chart courtesy of GrassrootsHealth:

According to 2011 National Center for Health Data statistics, nearly one in three Americans has vitamin D blood levels beneath 20 nanograms per milliliter (ng/ml). Remember, be wise when purchasing supplements. There is still debate over whether vitamin D3 is more effective than vitamin D2, but many recent studies are now leaning toward vitamin D3. In 2011, *The Journal of Clinical Endocrinology & Metabolism* found that D3 supplements were 87% more powerful in raising vitamin D levels in the blood compared to D2 supplements of the same dose. If you are unsure, consult your personal physician with regards to your blood test results, and make sure to also be a smart consumer. If you are truly purchasing vitamin D3, it will say "cholecalciferol" somewhere on the bottle or ingredients label. As of now, Consumer Reports gives Trader Joe's Vitamin D the nod. Just be wary that your blood levels are in the recommended range. And be wary of your children. Many of the conditions children are medicated for may simply be fixed through proper vitamin D intake.

Chapter 7 – The Skin Cancer Scare

Okay, so by now we've covered all the important bases. But there's still one giant, monster shadow looming over the sunspot of vitamin D. See, many people are afraid of vitamin D, despite all its benefits, because of one, disputable fact. *Too* much sun exposure is said to lead to skin cancer. This skin cancer scare is in part due to the paranoia instilled by dermatologists and sunblock producers. Although dermatologists are right in that too much sun will damage your skin and cause abnormalities, this does not mean that you should completely end your exposure to sun. In fact, many argue that vitamin D supplements simply cannot match the power of the all-natural star.

It's imperative to consider the varying ultraviolet radiation rays reaching the earth. UVA rays cause the most damage to skill and cell mutation. UVC rays are almost entirely stopped by the earth's atmosphere, and UVB rays are the ones that trigger the body's vitamin D intake process.

According to renowned Dr. Joseph Mercola, UV rays are not the problem when it comes to skin cancer. Just as recommended vitamin D levels have become more stringent with increased scientific scrutiny, so too have cancer and pre-cancer screenings. Nowadays, people are being diagnosed with melanoma skin cancer even when they only exhibit a minimal, non-malignant lesion. This has led many, like Dr. Mercola, to argue that the sun is not the main culprit in the increase in diagnoses.

Some experts argue that melanoma occurrence has actually been shown to decrease with increased sun exposure.

A study in Medical Hypotheses revealed that indoor workers have been exhibiting increased rates of melanoma since 1940. This is because they are behind windows, and are not receiving the UVB rays, only the UVA rays. Because the UVB rays enact the vitamin D intake process, indoor workers are missing out on their sunshine vitamin. Because many studies have shown vitamin D to fight cancer, outdoor workers receiving both UVB and UVA rays may actually have a lower risk of cancer—despite constant sun exposure.

At this point, it seems, the debate is still raging. Contradictory statements and studies continue to pour out, and agencies and companies with certain agendas continue to stick by their guns. Still, if your blood levels of vitamin D are in the recommended range, it's probably a good idea to use sunscreen at least some of the time. Especially if you burn easily.

For what it's worth, here is one sunscreen manufacturer, Banana Boat's, recommendations:

At the end of the day, natural change might be the best bet. If you or somebody you know is suffering from vitamin D deficiency, the most important thing to remember is lifestyle change. Eat healthier foods, get exercise in some sun, go for walks, talk to physicians, and learn everything about your body that you can. After all, it's your body, and you're the one living in it.

As science evolves, we will only know more. And the more we know, the more we realize one simple fact: every life needs a little sunshine.

A Special Note:

Thank you for reading *"Vitamin D Explained."* If you enjoyed reading this book and would like to read others similar to this, please do!

As always, thank you for reading.

And may you continue to live healthily and happily.

Sincerely,

C.K. Murray

Other works by C.K. Murray:

1. *Mindfulness Explained: The Mindful Solution to Stress, Depression, and Chronic Unhappiness*

2. *Emotional Intelligence Explained: How to Master Emotional Intelligence and Unlock Your True Ability*

3. *The Confidence Cure: Your Definitive Guide to Overcoming Low Self-Esteem, Learning Self-Love and Living Happily*